For Daddy, who taught us to never, ever let the turkeys get us down
—A.J.L.

To Rachel
—K.M.

THIS IS A BORZOI BOOK PUBLISHED BY ALFRED A. KNOPF

Text copyright © 2022 by Andrea J. Loney
Jacket art and interior illustrations copyright © 2022 by Keith Mallett

Picture credits (for page 43): Saks Fifth Avenue © David Deng/L.A. Conservancy;
Former Music Corporation of America (MCA) Building courtesy of the Art Museum of the University of Memphis;
Golden State Mutual Life Insurance Building courtesy of the Art Museum of the University of Memphis;
Theme Building at Los Angeles International Airport (LAX) © J. Paul Getty Trust. Getty Research Institute, Los Angeles;
Beverly Hills Hotel courtesy of the Art Museum of the University of Memphis

All rights reserved. Published in the United States by Alfred A. Knopf,
an imprint of Random House Children's Books, a division of Penguin Random House LLC, New York.

Knopf, Borzoi Books, and the colophon are registered trademarks of Penguin Random House LLC.

Visit us on the Web! rhcbooks.com

Educators and librarians, for a variety of teaching tools, visit us at RHTeachersLibrarians.com

Library of Congress Cataloging-in-Publication Data
Names: Loney, Andrea J, author. | Mallett, Keith, illustrator.
Title: Curve and flow: the elegant vision of L.A. architect Paul R. Williams / Andrea J. Loney, Keith Mallett.
Description: First edition. | New York: Alfred A. Knopf, [2022] | "This is a Borzoi book published by Alfred A. Knopf"—Colophon. |
Audience: Ages 4–8 | Summary: "A picture-book biography of L.A. architect Paul R. Williams."—Provided by publisher.
Identifiers: LCCN 2021039414 (print) | LCCN 2021039415 (ebook) |
ISBN 978-0-593-42907-5 (hardcover) | ISBN 978-0-593-42908-2 (library binding) | ISBN 978-0-593-42909-9 (ebook)
Subjects: LCSH: Williams, Paul R., 1894–1980—Juvenile literature. | Architects—United States—Biography—Juvenile literature. |
African American architects—Biography—Juvenile literature. | Los Angeles (Calif.)—Biography—Juvenile literature.
Classification: LCC NA737.W527 L66 2022 (print) | LCC NA737.W527 (ebook) | DDC 720.92 [B]—dc23

The text of this book is set in 16-point Brandon Grotesque Regular.
The illustrations were created digitally.
Book design by Nicole de las Heras

MANUFACTURED IN CHINA
10 9 8 7 6 5 4 3 2
First Edition

CURVE & FLOW

The Elegant Vision of L.A. Architect Paul R. Williams

Written by

Andrea J. Loney

Illustrated by

Keith Mallett

Alfred A. Knopf

New York

Long before the movie stars, fancy cars, and the Hollywood sign, Paul R. Williams makes his debut in a cozy home below a sunny Southern California sky.

On one of the oldest streets in Los Angeles, Paul and his brother watch their parents harvest the fruits of hard work and optimism. He learns that in the City of Angels, sometimes dreams come true.

But not always.
Before Paul turns five, he loses
his parents, and his brother is sent away.

But fate takes a curve, and love flows in.

At his new home, many of Paul's neighbors are immigrants. The children share food, stories, and languages from all over the world.

The sole Black child in his school, Paul likes learning with friends. But he really loves to draw and draw—especially buildings!

Paul gazes at the wide-open spaces of Los Angeles. From the curve of the San Gabriel Mountains to the flow of the Pacific Ocean, he imagines a breathtaking metropolis. He even dreams of building his own home.

"There are many famous Negro artists," says a family friend, "but I've never heard of a Negro architect."

Paul loves a challenge.

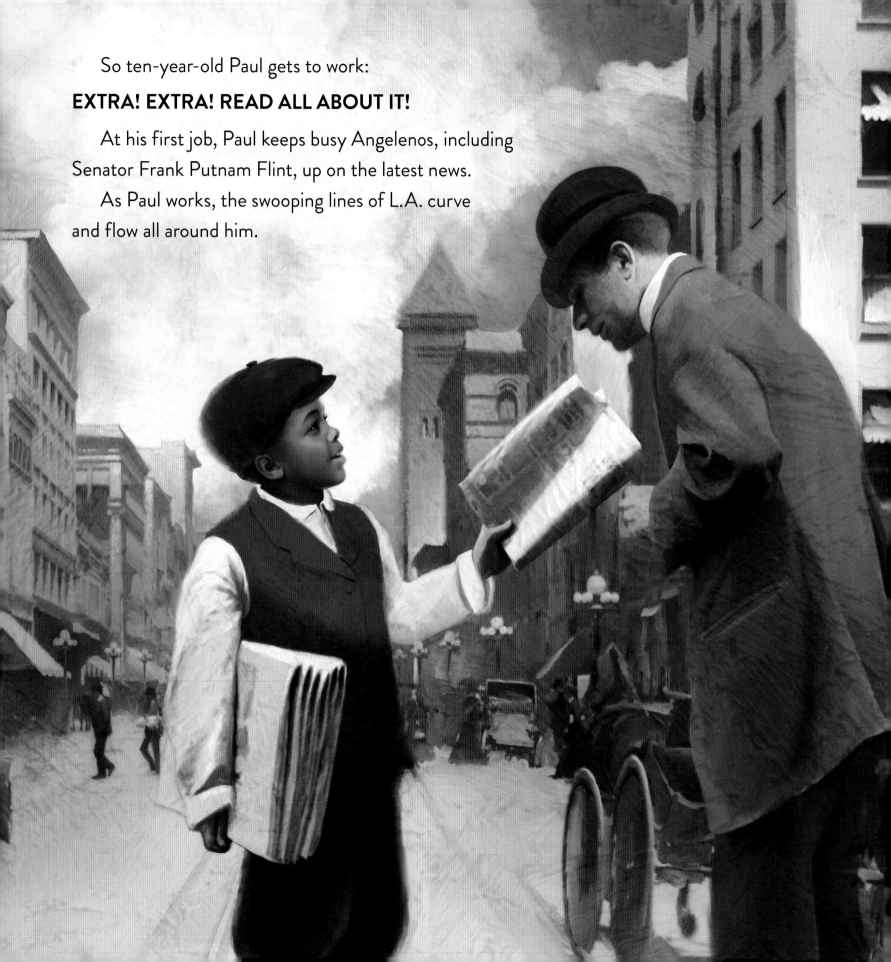

So ten-year-old Paul gets to work:

EXTRA! EXTRA! READ ALL ABOUT IT!

At his first job, Paul keeps busy Angelenos, including Senator Frank Putnam Flint, up on the latest news.

As Paul works, the swooping lines of L.A. curve and flow all around him.

At home, he draws and draws.

LIGHTS!
CAMERAS!
VROOOM!

While newfangled wonders captivate Paul's high school classmates, he concentrates on crafting his portfolio. Paul can see his future as clearly as a blueprint.

But not his guidance counselor.

"Who ever heard of a Negro architect?!"

In the early 1900s, most Black people can't buy fine houses or expensive buildings. The chances of a white man hiring Paul seem even slimmer.

The counselor begs Paul to study medicine or law—anything but architecture.

He doesn't even look at Paul's portfolio.

For the first time in Paul's life, he crashes right into the big stone wall of racism.

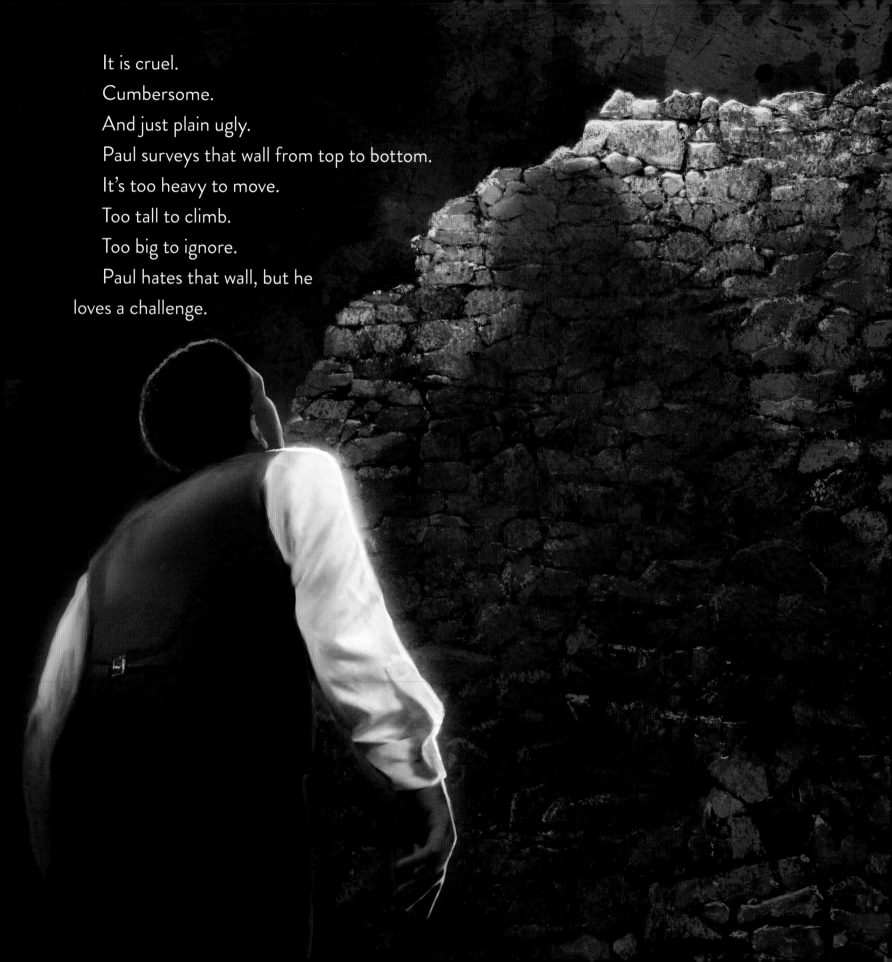

It is cruel.

Cumbersome.

And just plain ugly.

Paul surveys that wall from top to bottom.

It's too heavy to move.

Too tall to climb.

Too big to ignore.

Paul hates that wall, but he

loves a challenge.

Architects solve challenges all the time.

So Paul decides to take a curve and flow around that wall.

He maps out a blueprint for becoming such an exceptional artist, craftsman, and individual, people of all races will rush to hire Paul R. Williams, architect extraordinaire.

After graduation, Paul takes classes at five different schools, five nights a week. He studies the latest techniques . . .

. . . including one astounding skill that's sure to break down that stone wall of racism.

Paul has a knack for size and proportion—taking big, empty spaces and curving them into cozy nooks that connect in an easy flow.

He wins contest after contest with his clean and clever designs.

Next, after chasing twenty-five job leads, Paul joins one of the top architectural firms in the city.

Take that, stone wall!

At his new job, Paul learns how to design houses that showcase California's lovely weather and dazzling scenery. He takes structures from paper to pine to paint job. He also learns about a huge invisible wall of laws that blocks Black people from living in many parts of Los Angeles.

While Paul can create expensive $100,000 homes, he's not allowed to stay in them. In some towns, he has to leave before sundown.

Soon Paul finds his bride and sanctuary, the charming and stylish Della Mae Givens.

Finally, Paul has his own family again. But now they need a home.

So Della convinces Paul to enter three architectural contests at once.

But he doesn't win one—he wins them all!

With the prize money, they buy a small home in a Black working-class neighborhood in Los Angeles.

Paul and Della love entertaining friends there, but it's not like the houses Paul designs for his firm. It's not Paul's dream home. But sometimes dreams come true.

In 1921, Paul R. Williams becomes the first certified Black architect west of the Mississippi. To celebrate, an old classmate hires Paul to design a grand new estate in a new neighborhood with a familiar name.

His old customer Senator Flint pays Paul to design even more homes.

LIGHTS! CAMERAS! BUILDINGS!

With the money and prestige to open his own firm, Paul creates buildings for the Black community, young families, and even movie stars.

Sometimes Paul works with all-Black craftsmen.

Sometimes the white crews refuse to work with him.

But Paul finds ways to curve and flow around that big stone wall.

At the end of the 1920s, America takes a steep curve.

The stock market crashes.

The money disappears.

And Paul has many mouths to feed.

But opportunity flows in.

Mr. E. L. Cord, a wealthy automobile tycoon, wants to build a new mansion in Beverly Hills right away. But at their first meeting, the stone wall of racism rises between them.

Paul loves a challenge.

"I'll be back in twenty-four hours," Paul says.

He returns with the completed plans . . . and the special drawing technique he'd practiced to put nervous white clients at ease—and to turn Paul into a legend.

As Cord describes his vision, Paul draws and draws, sketching upside down and backward. Paul brings E. L. Cord's dream home to life right before his eyes.

The biggest names in Hollywood flock to the Cordhaven mansion in Beverly Hills. After that, they flock to Paul's office. The one and only Paul R. Williams becomes the celebrated "Architect to the Stars."

Paul's career skyrockets.

Just like his famous clients, Paul's creations are classic, bold, dazzling, innovative, and unforgettable.

But what about Paul's dream home?
He's got all the money he needs. He knows *exactly* what he wants.
But there are dreams and then there are laws.

The Beverly Hills Hotel even hires Paul to redesign the Polo Lounge and the Fountain Coffee Room. Once the paint dries, Paul could marvel at his signature achievement—the building sign is even printed in his own distinctive handwriting. But could Paul stop by for a milkshake with Della or their daughters?

No.

Once again, Paul can enter the building as the architect, but not as a Black person. No matter how high Paul rises, the stone wall of racism grinds against his face.

But he still believes that in the City of Angels, sometimes dreams come true.
And Paul loves a challenge.

This time, Paul takes a sharp curve and flows in a different direction.

He trades blueprints for banking.

With local business partners and friends, Paul starts a bank for the Black community. Instead of dealing with traditional lenders that often say no, the Black people of Los Angeles could finally raise funds for their own churches, businesses, and homes. All across South L.A., dreams come true.

Soon after, the U.S. Supreme Court stops supporting the contract covenants that shut Black people out of neighborhoods across the country. Finally, Paul is free to build his most beloved creation of all.

Under a sunny Southern California sky, in the elegant Los Angeles neighborhood of Lafayette Square, Paul R. Williams constructs a gorgeous dwelling that curves and flows, delights and comforts. It is his masterpiece. Paul and Della are home at last.

For the rest of their lives, Paul and Della enjoy sharing their dream home with family and friends. Paul continues designing homes, churches, hospitals, and more. The classic L.A. style of the 1950s and '60s reflects his vision. By the time he retires in 1973, Paul Revere Williams has created more than 3,000 structures all over the world.

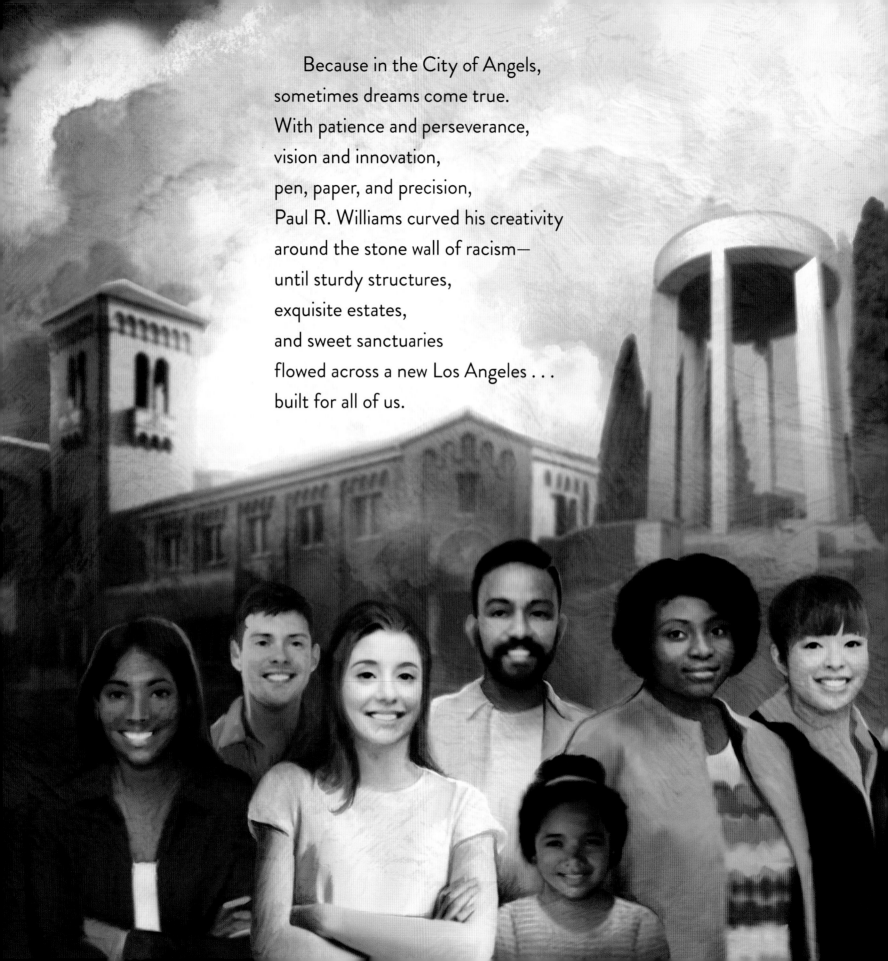

Because in the City of Angels,
sometimes dreams come true.
With patience and perseverance,
vision and innovation,
pen, paper, and precision,
Paul R. Williams curved his creativity
around the stone wall of racism—
until sturdy structures,
exquisite estates,
and sweet sanctuaries
flowed across a new Los Angeles . . .
built for all of us.

AUTHOR'S NOTE

While researching this book, I checked the history of our own home, built in 1924 in the L.A. County city of Inglewood. The original deed says only "Caucasians," or white people, can live here. So back then, I wouldn't have been allowed to sit at this desk, where I'm writing these words right now, simply because I'm a Black person. What a chilling thought! Then I wondered how Paul must've felt as he created magnificent houses, which he himself was forbidden to own.

Even though Los Angeles has long been known for its open-mindedness and diversity, many barriers have kept Black people from moving to certain parts of the county. In some areas called "sundown towns," locals or the police could force Black people to leave before sunset. Covenant clauses in housing deeds forbade Black people, and sometimes other racial or religious minorities, from living in some homes. In a practice called "redlining," banks refused to lend money for housing to Black people in specific areas of town. And after World War II, the G.I. Bill gave money for new homes to returning veterans, but not to most Black veterans—even though they'd fought in the same war.

These discriminatory practices, however, were not unique to Los Angeles—they took place in communities across the United States.

Of course, Paul R. Williams was keenly aware of these injustices. But he loved his work. He loved seeing dreams come true. And when racism blocked his path, he found ingenious ways to curve and flow around it as he focused on his goal of making a better Los Angeles for everyone. I wrote this book in hopes of bringing greater recognition to this extraordinary individual, whose works are woven through our everyday lives here in L.A., and whose mission endlessly inspires me. I hope he inspires you, too.

SELECTED SOURCES

Bond, Max. "Still Here." *Harvard Design Magazine*, no. 2. harvarddesignmagazine.org/issues/2/still-here

Hudson, Karen E. *Paul R. Williams, Architect.* New York: Rizzoli, 1993.

Hudson, Karen E. *Paul R. Williams, Architect: A Legacy of Style.* New York: Rizzoli, 2000.

Hudson, Karen E. *Paul R. Williams: Classic Hollywood Style.* New York: Rizzoli, 2012.

The Paul Revere Williams Project. paulrwilliamsproject.org/

Trufelman, Avery, producer. "The Architect of Hollywood." 99percentinvisible.org/episode/the-architect-of-hollywood

Williams, Paul R. "I Am a Negro." *American Magazine*, July 1937.

PHOTOS

Saks Fifth Avenue | Collaborating with two other architects, Paul designed the opulent exterior and cozy interiors for a peaceful shopping experience.

Former Music Corporation of America (MCA) Building | One of Paul's proudest achievements, the original MCA headquarters building was created for "agent to the stars" Jules Caesar Stein.

Golden State Mutual Life Insurance Building | Home to one of the first companies offering life insurance to Black Los Angelenos, this building featured huge murals showing the history of African Americans in California from 1781 to 1949.

Beverly Hills Hotel | Paul's additions and renovations to this iconic Los Angeles landmark defined the glamorous Los Angeles experience for hotel visitors from around the world.

Theme Building at Los Angeles International Airport (LAX) | Paul joined the architectural team that modernized LAX. This famous photo depicts the visionary spirit of the project, although he didn't design this specific structure.

TIMELINE

The current Los Angeles area is home to the Chumash and Tongva Native American people.

1781 Fourteen families of Native American, African, and European background start a farming community near what is now the Los Angeles River. Over time, the area is claimed by Spain, Mexico, and, in 1850, by the U.S.A.

1890 Paul Revere Williams's parents, Chester and Lila Williams, and their son, Chester Jr., move to Downtown Los Angeles from Tennessee.

1894 Paul is born February 18 on Santee Street in Downtown Los Angeles.

1896 His father, who ran a fruit cart on Olvera Street, dies of tuberculosis at 31. Two years later, his mother dies of a lung disease at 34.

1899 Paul's older brother, Chester Jr., is sent to live with another family. Four-year-old Paul is cared for by Emily and Charles Clarkson, who are family friends from First A.M.E. Church.

1900 Paul attends Sentous Avenue Grammar School.

1908 Ford produces the first Model T automobile.

1912 Paul graduates from Polytechnic School, then attends Los Angeles School of Art and Design and the Beaux-Arts Institute of Design Atelier.

1913 Paul works for landscape architect Wilbur D. Cook, Jr.

1914 Paul works for architect Reginald Davis Johnson on California-style luxury homes until 1917.

1915 Paul is certified as a building contractor.

1916 Paul enrolls at USC as one of eight students studying architectural engineering. He graduates in 1919.

1917 Paul marries Della Mae Givens.

1920 Paul and Della move to West 35th St. in South Central L.A.
Paul is appointed to the first City Planning Commission of Los Angeles, serving until 1928.

1921 Paul works for architect John C. Austin. He helps prepare the drawings of the Shrine Civic Auditorium and the Hollywood Masonic Temple.
Paul is the first Black man west of the Mississippi licensed to practice architecture.
His friend Louis Cass asks him to design a new home. Then Senator Frank Putnam Flint asks him to design several homes in his new development.

1923 The Hollywoodland sign is erected.
Paul establishes his own firm, Paul R. Williams and Associates.
Paul is the first Black member of the American Institute of Architects (AIA).

1924 Paul designs the Second Baptist Church and the Conner-Johnson Mortuary. He designs the 28th St. YMCA—the first YMCA built for Black children.

1928 Paul starts designing homes for famous silent-film actor Lon Chaney, Sr.

1929 The stock market crashes and the Great Depression follows.

1933 Paul creates E. L. Cord's magnificent new home, Cordhaven.
Mayor Frank Shaw appoints Paul to the first Los Angeles Housing Commission, where he serves until 1941.

1935 Paul is licensed to practice in Washington, D.C. With Black architect Hilyard Robinson, he designs Langston Terrace, the first federally funded public housing project in the country.

1940 Paul designs the Roosevelt Naval Base in Long Beach, California.

1941 Paul opens an office in Bogotá, Colombia.
The United States joins World War II.

1942 Paul designs housing units for soldiers at Fort Huachuca in Arizona.

1945 Paul publishes his first book, *The Small Home of Tomorrow,* to help veterans build their own homes. The next year he publishes *New Homes for Today.*

1947 Paul becomes vice president and director of Broadway Federal Savings and Loan, a federal bank created by African Americans to serve the local Black community.
Governor Earl Warren appoints Paul to the California Redevelopment Commission.

1948 The U.S. Supreme Court strikes down laws protecting restrictive housing covenants.

1949 Paul designs a wing of the Beverly Hills Hotel, including the Polo Lounge and Fountain Coffee Room.

1950 Paul becomes an associate architect on the United Nations Building in Paris.

1952 Paul finally builds his own dream home in Lafayette Square, an upscale neighborhood in Los Angeles.

1953 President Eisenhower appoints Paul to the National Housing Commission. Paul is awarded the NAACP Spingarn Medal.

1957 Paul is the first African American inducted into the AIA College of Fellows. He wins the Los Angeles Area Chamber of Commerce Award for Creative Planning for his work on singer Frank Sinatra's house.

1961 With Hilyard Robinson, Paul designs the new Engineering and Architecture Building at Howard University.
Paul designs St. Jude's Children's Research Hospital in Tennessee.
Along with other notable architects, Paul joins the Los Angeles Jet Age Terminal construction project to renovate L.A. International Airport.

1964 Paul receives an honorary doctorate from Atlanta University. At this point he has received honorary doctorates from the Tuskegee Institute (1956), Howard University (1952), and Lincoln University in Missouri (1941). He's licensed to practice in Nevada.

1973 Paul retires. The next year he becomes AIA Emeritus.

1980 Paul dies of diabetes on January 23 in Los Angeles at age 85.

1992 The office containing Paul's files is destroyed by arson during the Los Angeles riots. It's assumed that the majority of his records are lost.

2017 Paul is posthumously awarded the AIA Gold Medal, presented by Black architect Phil Freelon, designer of the Smithsonian National Museum of African American History and Culture.

2020 Over 40,000 of Paul's surviving papers, including building plans, blueprints, photos, drawings, and more are discovered by Paul's granddaughter Karen E. Hudson and donated to the University of Southern California School of Architecture and the Getty Research Institute for their archive.
PBS airs the documentary *Hollywood's Architect: The Paul R. Williams Story.*

ACKNOWLEDGMENTS

I am so grateful to these individuals and organizations for helping me bring this story to life: Sharon of Children's Book World for the initial inspiration, and Julia Wasson for the endless encouragement. Michelle Markel's picture-book nonfiction class. L.A. readers Benson Shum, Cassandra Federman, Colleen Paeff, Donn Swaby, Jennie Palmer, Karen English, Krista Whittemore, Maureen Charles, Sue Berger, Sue Ganz-Schmitt, and Zeena Pliska. East Coast readers Cheryl Keely and Katey Howes, and my nieces Eden, Lilly, and Hannah Bazelais. Our creative dream team—editor Erin Clarke, art editor Nicole de las Heras, copy editor Artie Bennett, and illustrator Keith Mallett. My agent, Andrea Cascardi. The Los Angeles and Santa Monica public libraries, the Paul Revere Williams Project, and the Los Angeles Conservancy. My Christopher; my mom, Phyllis Slaten; and my late mother-in-love, Dorothy Schwarz, for their steadfast support. And finally, Karen E. Hudson for preserving her grandfather's legacy for generations to come.